Original title:
Art of the Heart

Copyright © 2024 Swan Charm
All rights reserved.

Editor: Jessica Elisabeth Luik
Author: Olivia Orav
ISBN HARDBACK: 978-9916-86-300-8
ISBN PAPERBACK: 978-9916-86-301-5

Sentimental Scribe

Pages whisper secrets,
In the quiet of the night.
Words dance with emotions,
Under the soft moonlight.

Pens ink stories past,
Echoes of a heart's plight.
Time etches memories,
In the scribe's tender sight.

Love lingers in phrases,
A solace so contrived.
Each stroke, a silent promise,
In sentiments revived.

Aurora of Emotions

Heartbeats paint the sky,
With hues of joy and sorrow.
Twilight dreams converge,
On the palette of tomorrow.

Tears mix with laughter,
In twilight's deep embrace.
Emotions rise like dawn,
In an ever-changing space.

Nights cloak our desires,
Shadows shade our fears.
Auroras burst within us,
Lighting up the years.

Inked Intimacies

Love's ink traces outlines,
On a canvas of skin.
Secrets scripted softly,
Where passions begin.

Eyes whisper stories,
Lips recite the prose.
Each touch, a paragraph,
In a tale that ever grows.

Moments swell like verses,
In a lover's diary.
Each kiss, a line of poetry,
In intimate reverie.

Prismatic Pulchritude

Beauty shifts in light,
As prism captures glance.
Colors blend and fracture,
In an endless dance.

Eyes find hidden worlds,
In a spectrum vast and true.
Hearts interpret visions,
In shades of every hue.

Glimmers of existence,
Through prisms we perceive.
Pulchritude prismatic,
In the soul's reflect to weave.

Acrylic Affections

In strokes of passion bold and bright,
Our vivid dreams take flight, ignite,
A canvas wide with hues so true,
Reflects the hearts of me and you.

The palette whispers tales we weave,
In every swish, in each reprieve,
Colors blend in tender sway,
Binding love in bold array.

Cadmium love and cobalt skies,
Capture moments, close your eyes,
Acrylic depths hold secrets dear,
In layered strokes, we conquer fear.

When morning's light meets twilight's gleam,
Our painted love, a waking dream,
Acrylic threads of life entwine,
In every shade, with love divine.

Watercolor Whispers

Soft and gentle, wash of blue,
Whispers of the dawn anew,
In fleeting strokes, emotions bloom,
A watercolor's subtle plume.

Each drop of paint, a liquid sigh,
As shadows blend and shapes belie,
In pools of light, our secrets rest,
A tender heart, a gentle crest.

Cerulean words, in twilight shared,
Soft confessions, unprepared,
Translucent hues, in love's embrace,
Watercolor whispers trace.

Let flow the rivers, let them seek,
Our whispered love, both bold and meek,
In every stain, a promise calls,
Watercolor whispers fall.

Sketches of Sentiment

In pencil lines, our story grows,
Each stroke a pulse, emotion shows,
Shaded whispers, soft and grand,
Sketches of our hearts in hand.

Graphite dreams and shadows cast,
From present moments to the past,
In lines so pure, our spirits blend,
Sketches of the love we send.

Each erasure, not a wound,
But places where new hopes are tuned,
In every curve, a tale unfolds,
Sentiments in pencil told.

From dusty sketches, memories rise,
In every mark, a sweet surprise,
With pencil's kiss, our love surrounds,
Sketches of sentiment unbound.

Mosaic of Memories

Piece by piece, we carve our past,
In shattered bits, our love will last,
A mosaic bright with colors scheme,
Reflecting every shared dream.

Fragments born of time's embrace,
Each piece a love we can't erase,
In every shard, a life revealed,
Our broken hearts, together healed.

Emerald glows with sapphire hue,
Memories stitched of me and you,
With every glance, a spark ignites,
In pieces small, together tight.

Our mosaic of memories stand,
A testament of hand in hand,
Forever fixed, our hearts align,
In colored shards, our souls combine.

Lyrical Layers

Beneath the sky of endless blue,
Dreams unfurl like morning dew,
Whispers soft in twilight's keep,
Secrets that the shadows sweep.

Echoes dance in moonlight's gaze,
Drawing paths through night's embrace,
Songs unsung in silent grace,
Winds that trace a fleeting face.

Stars ignite the darkened sea,
Luminaries wild and free,
Smiles hidden in the breeze,
Wonders that the heart can seize.

Heartfelt Hues

In a world of vibrant shade,
Love and longing gently laid,
Colors blend where hearts collide,
Brushstrokes where emotions bide.

Emerald dreams in sapphire skies,
Whispered truths and tender lies,
Blush of dusk and dawn's first light,
Canvas painted through the night.

Crimson echoes of a kiss,
Fleeting moments wrapped in bliss,
Palette rich with teardrop rain,
Every shade a hint of pain.

Graffiti of Feelings

On the walls of silent streets,
Murals made where heartbeats meet,
Spray of hope and splash of fear,
Art that only spirits hear.

Vivid strokes of joy and rage,
Chapters scrawled on concrete page,
Every tag a name untold,
Histories in colors bold.

Lines that twist and shapes that bend,
Messages that start and end,
In the urban dusk they fade,
Love's graffiti, memories made.

Easel of Emotions

On the easel, life's parade,
Every brush each tear and shade,
Journeys through the soul's terrain,
Portraits of both joy and pain.

Mixing hues of lost and found,
Silence painted, echo's sound,
Shadows shift in gentle hue,
Heart's own portrait, ever true.

Canvas whispers, strokes that tell,
Dreams embraced where nightwinds dwell,
Easel holds emotions deep,
Art that wakes while shadows sleep.

Luminous Gazes

Beneath the twilight's gentle haze,
Stars reflect in tranquil maze,
Eyes that meet with silent praise,
And kindle dreams through endless days.

A whisper threads the evening air,
Soft as shadows, bright and rare,
In each glance a story shared,
Bound by light, beyond compare.

Glimmering orbs of night unfold,
Tales of love in whispers told,
In their depths, a mystery old,
Luminous gazes, hearts of gold.

With every glance, a universe,
Silent vows in soft converse,
They navigate the wide disperse,
Boundless realms in verse and verse.

Through the dark, their beams align,
Drawing paths, a fate's design,
In their light, our souls refine,
Luminous gazes, pure and divine.

Magnetic Meanderings

Through labyrinths of heart and mind,
Paths obscure, yet intertwined,
Silent forces undefined,
Magnetic pulls that bind the blind.

Wandering souls in cosmic dance,
Led by currents, chance to chance,
Unseen hands adjust the stance,
Drawing near by some romance.

In the flux and ebb of tides,
Swirling depths where truth abides,
Hidden pulls where love resides,
Meandering hearts, no guide provides.

Each step forward, a mystery,
In the web of what will be,
Pulled together endlessly,
By invisible decree.

Ever drawn, our destinies,
Through the darkened galaxies,
Bound by unseen entities,
Magnetic, in our journeys.

Yearnings in Color

In hues of dawn, desires blaze,
Soft pastels of morning raise,
Yearnings bloom in bright arrays,
Life painted in a thousand ways.

Crimson whispers, passion's call,
Deep within, the heart's enthrall,
Echoes rise and gently fall,
Coloring our inner wall.

Azure dreams in daylight gleam,
Floating on a lazy stream,
Soft the shades of love esteem,
Yearnings weave in endless seam.

In twilight's fold, the shadows play,
Violet sighs embrace the day,
Hope in every shade of gray,
Sketching dreams in gentle sway.

Each desire, a vibrant tone,
In the canvas of unknown,
Yearnings in the colors shown,
In our hearts, a vivid home.

Vivid Rhythms

In the pulse of morning light,
Rhythms dance, so pure and bright,
Vivid beats in gentle sight,
Awakening the silent night.

Whispers in the breezes flow,
Melodies both soft and slow,
Life in every beat does grow,
Songs of time in endless row.

Echoes in the heartbeats found,
Resonance in every sound,
Vivid rhythms all around,
In the silence, we are bound.

Harmonies of life and soul,
In each sound, we find our role,
Together making pieces whole,
Rhythms vivid, hearts console.

From the dawn to evening's fall,
Songs that bind us, one and all,
Heartbeats answer to the call,
In vivid rhythms, we enthrall.

Ink of Aflutter

In whispers of ink, a tale unfolds,
Where butterflies dance, and time beholds.
Their wings, a flicker in twilight's beam,
A canvas alight with every dream.

Aflutter they float, on breezes so light,
Through dusk and dawn, in day and night.
Their colors weave in poetic strands,
Etched by a writer's tender hands.

Between each page, their spirits soar,
From ancient lore to futures more.
Ink and wings, a timeless pair,
In realms of thought, they freely fare.

As words disperse in winds anew,
They find their place in skies of blue.
Bound by ink, yet free they lie,
In realms where only muses fly.

Radiant Reverie

In the amber glow of sundown's grace,
Dreams awaken, time's sweet embrace.
Under the hues of twilight's sheen,
Radiant reveries softly glean.

Stars like whispers adorn the night,
A symphony cast in silver light.
Each dawn and dusk, a fleeting muse,
In cosmic ballet, our hearts to choose.

Moonlit rivers of thoughts entwine,
In harmony, the world aligns.
Cradled in the night's gentle palm,
We find our reverie, tender and calm.

Through realms that only dreams unveil,
Our spirits sail, with wings so frail.
In painted skies, with hope we steer,
To where the radiant visions clear.

Strokes of Affection

Brush of love, on canvas bare,
Crafting moments, tender care.
In every stroke, a story told,
Of hearts entwined, and dreams of gold.

Colors blend in soft embrace,
Each hue a kiss, a warm solace.
From dawn's blush to twilight's hue,
Affection's dance, a vibrant view.

Palette of passion, shades of grace,
A masterpiece in love's own space.
No word or song could e'er convey,
The depth in strokes we weave each day.

In every curve and gentle line,
A testament to love divine.
Unseen by eyes but felt so deep,
A love that promises to keep.

Tones of Tenderness

Whispers of wind through autumn leaves,
Softly sing of love's reprieves.
Each note, a tender, fleeting breeze,
In harmony, our hearts find ease.

Melodies weave through twilight's veil,
Where soft embraces never fail.
In every chord, a sweet caress,
The symphony of tenderness.

Echoes of love in silent nights,
Hold us close in gentle flights.
The moon, our witness, serene and mild,
To tones of tenderness, so undefiled.

Through symphonies of night and day,
Our souls in music, find their way.
In every whispered note, we find,
The timeless bond our hearts have twined.

Harmonies in Hue

Soft whispers of blue in the morning sky,
Blushing roses greet the dawn's amber glow.
Emerald meadows where butterflies fly,
The world awakens with colors that flow.

Golden hues dance on rippling streams,
Lavender whispers in fields far and wide.
Crimson twilight and translucent dreams,
The canvas of day where shades coincide.

Cerulean depths where sunlight dips,
Tangerine hues in the evening light.
A spectrum of wonders, the earth slowly sips,
Nature's palette, a truly wondrous sight.

Tender Verses

Whispered dreams in the quiet night,
Moonlit paths where hearts quietly meet.
Gentle hands in tender light,
Soft murmurs of love, so deep, so sweet.

Silent vows beneath the stars,
Eyes that speak a thousand words.
In the hush, where nothing mars,
The tender song of love is heard.

Eternal bonds that time can't sever,
Hearts entwined as moments blend.
A love that lives in dreams forever,
A poem of souls that never end.

Vivid Reverberations

Echoes of laughter in sunlit spaces,
Ripples on water, a timeless dance.
Footsteps imprint on nature's traces,
Moments of joy in every glance.

Birdsong drifting on morning breezes,
Mountain peaks where eagles soar.
The hum of life as daylight teases,
Nature's symphony, forevermore.

Wind through trees in quiet whispers,
Rain's soft patter on old tin roofs.
The heartbeat of the earth that lingers,
The vivid pulse of life's own truths.

Heartfelt Harmony

Threads of melody in heartfelt song,
Notes of love that gently blend.
In the symphony, where hearts belong,
Harmony's hand as souls transcend.

Strings of fate in chords of gold,
Tunes that wrap in warm embrace.
Every measure, a story told,
Eternal music through time and space.

Rhythms found in life's own beat,
Cadences that softly sway.
A harmony pure, alive, replete,
A loving tune that guides our way.

Gilded Love

In fields of gold, our hearts did meet,
A love so pure, so rare and sweet.
With every smile, the days turned bright,
Together, we soared to endless height.

Underneath the mystic, twinkling sky,
We promised never to say goodbye.
Through storms and calm, we stand as one,
Gilded love, our race well-run.

A touch, a whisper, mutual embrace,
In your arms, my sacred place.
The moonbeams dance upon our dreams,
Love's brilliant light, forever gleams.

Flourishes of Fondness

Beneath the canopy of cherry trees,
Affection blossoms in the breeze.
Unspoken words, in glances shared,
A love so tender, beyond compare.

Moments woven in the fabric of time,
Every heartbeat, a gentle rhyme.
In laughter, tears, and silent sighs,
Fondness flourishes, never dies.

Whispers carried by the evening tide,
In your warmth, I find my guide.
Together, we'll rise above the storm,
In fondness, our spirits transform.

Anatomy of Affection

Within the chest, where love resides,
A pulse that sparkles, never hides.
With every breath and heartbeat's sound,
Affection's roots grow deep, profound.

Muscles tighten, senses keen,
In tender moments, love is seen.
An intricate weave of touch and soul,
Two halves uniting, becoming whole.

Eyes that speak a thousand tales,
Lips that write love's sacred trails.
In every gesture, large or small,
Affection's anatomy, we heed its call.

Pigments of Passion

In the canvas of our intertwined fate,
Strokes of passion, vivid and great.
Colors blend in fiery embrace,
Every touch, a trace of grace.

Crimson whispers in shadows deep,
In passion's wake, no promises cheap.
The palette of love's endless hue,
Every shade, tender and true.

With each caress, a masterpiece forged,
In hearts and dreams, passion is gorge.
Our love, a painting, timelessly grand,
Pigments of passion, cherished and planned.

Illuminated Affection

In twilight's gentle, amber glow,
Our hearts find solace, sweet, and slow.
Whispers of love, like breezes play,
Guiding us through night to day.

Stars above reflect our gaze,
In tender light, our spirits blaze.
Bound by threads of cosmic might,
Our love transcends the pale of night.

In every touch, in every glance,
There's magic in our fateful dance.
Through shadows cast and dreams aloft,
Your love remains my guiding loft.

Illuminated by the heart,
We wander, never far apart.
In worlds unseen, our spirits soar,
Together, now and evermore.

In twilight's hush, our souls align,
With you, dear heart, the stars align.
Through trials, tears, and laughter shared,
Our bond of light, forever dared.

Confetti of Compassion

In moments fleeting, small and bright,
Acts of kindness paint the night.
Gentle words, like colored rain,
Ease the burden, soothe the pain.

Hearts that open, unafraid,
Scatter love where shadows fade.
Confetti falls, a tender bliss,
In every smile, in every kiss.

Through hardships fierce, and valleys deep,
Compassion sows what we shall reap.
Every gesture, grand or small,
A testament to love's sweet call.

In crowded streets, in empty rooms,
Our kindness like a flower blooms.
A simple touch, a listening ear,
Can make the world a place sincere.

With every step, a chance to show,
A love that blooms and freely grows.
In confetti's gentle, joyful flight,
We find our shared and pure delight.

Pastel Promises

In morning's blush, the sky unfolds,
Soft hues of pink, of blue, of gold.
A symphony of light and air,
In pastel shades, a love we share.

With every dawn, new hopes arise,
Painted in the boundless skies.
Promises in whispers made,
In gentle colors, never fade.

A tender vow, a sweet embrace,
In hues that time will not erase.
Our dreams, like clouds, in softest white,
Merge and dance in pure delight.

Through seasons' change, our bond remains,
In pastel hues, we ease the pains.
In storms and sun, in joy and woe,
Our love in gentle strokes will glow.

In every heart, a painter's hand,
Crafts promises that gold withstand.
With every dawn, our love renews,
In pastel promises, our truths.

Cameos of Connection

In fleeting moments, life does weave,
A tapestry that hearts believe.
Small cameos of joy and pain,
Connections found in loss and gain.

A glance, a touch, a word unspoken,
In these, our human bonds are woken.
Through time and space, our spirits meet,
In cameo, our souls complete.

Each little scene, a precious part,
Of greater narratives in heart.
In memories' soft, enduring light,
We find our way through darkest night.

In laughter shared and tears that fall,
We heed the universal call.
Through fleeting frames, we see so clear,
The essence of our presence here.

In every face, in every heart,
A cameo, a vital part.
Connections forged in life's brief span,
Revealing all that's shared by man.

Pictorial Passions

In canvas vast, the colors play,
A dance of hues, both night and day.
Each stroke a whisper, soft and light,
In shadows deep, in morning's bright.

Eyes trace the arcs of brush's flight,
A symphony in black and white.
Passions bloom in every frame,
Love and sorrow, fire and flame.

Textures, tones, a world unfurls,
Silent stories, hearts in curls.
Ink and oil, they blend, they merge,
Drawing dreams on passion's surge.

In stillness found, in chaos too,
Hues of red and tranquil blue.
Each moment captured, ever new,
A world reborn, a vibrant view.

Hope and heartache intertwined,
On paper, they forever bind.
A graphic tale for eyes to see,
In art, we're ever truly free.

Brush of Destiny

A blank slate waits, so pure and fair,
The artist's heart, the painter's care.
Destiny in every stroke,
Life and dreams in lines evoke.

With brush in hand, fate's path begins,
Colorful tales, they weave and spin.
A future seen in hues unwound,
Destiny in shades profound.

Each bristle kissed by fate's tender sigh,
The world unfolds as ink will dry.
A tapestry of time and space,
In art, we find our destined place.

The brush, a compass to the soul,
Tracing paths, making us whole.
An artist's dream, a fateful quest,
In every stroke, our true bequest.

From light's embrace to shadow's end,
Our stories on the canvas blend.
In art, our destinies align,
A future found in every line.

Ember of Emotions

In the heart's quiet, embers glow,
Feelings light, yet dark and slow.
Whispers in the silence found,
Emotions in the soul abound.

A shimmer soft of joy and pain,
Love and loss, a sweet refrain.
Flickers in the deepest night,
Guiding through the endless plight.

In every smile, in every tear,
Embers of emotions near.
Burning bright or fading swift,
In each heart, a timeless gift.

In laughter's burst and sorrow's cry,
A flame that never says goodbye.
Gently swaying, softly burn,
Emotions in their silent turn.

Hope's faint glow, despair's bright flame,
Love's warm light, and guilt's cold shame.
Each an ember, small but grand,
In the heart, they firmly stand.

Timeless Sonata

A melody in the still of night,
Stars above and heart's delight.
In echoes vast, the notes take flight,
A timeless tune of purest light.

Piano keys in moon's soft glow,
A song of old, yet new to know.
In every chord, a story spun,
Of dreams and love and setting sun.

Strings that weep and voices sing,
Of whispered hopes, of joys they bring.
In harmony, the soul's refrain,
A sonata in timeless gain.

Rhythms beat like heartbeats near,
In music's arms, we lose our fear.
Each measure, every fleeting note,
A timeless tale in every quote.

From dawn's embrace to twilight's hue,
A song eternal, always true.
In melodies, our hearts reside,
In music's waves, we ever glide.

Heartstrings and Hues

A canvas stretched, the hues collide,
In brilliant strokes, emotions glide,
Each color whispers, heart's secret hues,
A symphony painted, in vibrant clues.

The brushstrokes dance, in wild array,
Soft pastels to bold, they sway,
In every tint, a tale untold,
Heartstrings play, in shades of gold.

A crimson blush, a lover's cry,
In twilight's glow, a gentle sigh,
The canvas holds what words conceal,
A masterpiece of depths we feel.

In every smear, a hope renewed,
In every blend, a promise brewed,
The hues of love, so deep, profound,
Heartstrings plucked by colors found.

From dawn till dusk, the palette burns,
In every shade, a heart returns,
To where the art and soul unite,
In hues that cast the darkest night.

Palette of Passion

With every stroke, the colors merge,
In passions deep, they seek to surge,
A vibrant clash of fire and ice,
The palette mixed, a lover's vice.

A whisper soft, a shout so bold,
In shades of red, a story told,
The canvas breathes with every hue,
A tale of love, forever true.

In purple dusk and amber dawn,
The fleeting moments linger on,
Each color paints a memory,
A silent song, a sweet reverie.

Beneath the stars, the pigments blend,
In every tone, a heart to mend,
A brush of love on canvas laid,
A masterpiece in twilight shade.

Through every line, a passion flows,
In every hue, it deeply shows,
The palette rich with love's embrace,
In painted strokes, two hearts replace.

Silent Sonatas

A tune unheard, yet deeply felt,
In silent notes, emotions melt,
The sonata plays, in whispers bright,
A symphony of endless night.

Each note a touch, a fleeting kiss,
In melodies of tender bliss,
The silence speaks in heart's refrain,
A song of love in quiet pain.

In pauses deep, the echoes cry,
In silent weeps, the moments lie,
A sonata of the lost and found,
In voiceless chords, a love unbound.

The music sways in ghostly light,
A shadowed waltz in purest white,
In quietude, the heart relays,
A sonata of the whispered gaze.

Let silence be the guiding hand,
In music's arms, the heartstrings stand,
A silent sonata, pure and true,
A symphony of me and you.

Visions in Crimson

In crimson dreams, the visions dance,
A fervent gaze, a stolen glance,
The deepest red of passion's fire,
In every hue, a deep desire.

The moonlight bathes in scarlet hues,
In silken threads, a dream pursues,
A tapestry of love's embrace,
In crimson light, we find our place.

Through crimson tides of dawn's first light,
The dreams cascade in endless flight,
Each vision holds a world anew,
In shades of red, our love grew.

With every beat, the heart beats red,
In crimson flows, our paths have led,
A journey painted in desire,
In scarlet dreams, our souls conspire.

The visions merge in blazing flame,
In crimson love, we'll stake our claim,
To find in every ardent kiss,
A world in red, eternal bliss.

Ephemeral Muse

In twilight's gentle, fleeting grace,
The muse alights, a whispered trace,
Of dreams that dance on transient breeze,
And time that flows with quiet ease.

She weaves the dusk, with hues untold,
In shadows' arms, her secrets hold,
A moment's breath, a sigh's embrace,
Then vanishes without a trace.

The stars ignite in silent plea,
To capture fragments, set them free,
But fleeting is her tender rhyme,
A wisp of thought, a fleeting chime.

In moonlit night, her song persists,
Yet fades within the morning mists,
Ephemeral, she drifts away,
A soft allure, that cannot stay.

So cherish well her whispered song,
For she is gone before too long,
An echo in the evening hue,
Ephemeral, and always new.

Painted Whispers

Upon the canvas, whispers play,
In strokes of light and shadow's sway,
A symphony in colors bright,
Emerging from the depths of night.

The artist's hand, so deftly moves,
To capture what the soul behooves,
In hues of blue, and gold, and red,
A story in each line is said.

Through every brush, a world unfolds,
Of whispered dreams and tales untold,
The silence of the paint reveals,
The deepest thoughts, the heart conceals.

In every hue a voice is found,
In silence, colors do resound,
A whisper in the still of day,
In painted form, they softly say.

Oh, listen close to each fine line,
The whispers of the heart, divine,
In every stroke, a breath of life,
Painted whispers, free of strife.

Echoes of the Heartbeat

In silence deep, a heartbeat's sound,
An echo in the dark, profound,
It whispers secrets to the night,
In rhythm's pulse, a soft delight.

Each beat, a story gently told,
Of love and life, so brave, so bold,
In echoes warm, the past remains,
And through the heart, the essence reigns.

In every pulse, a memory lies,
Of laughing eyes and tearful skies,
A symphony within the chest,
The heart's own song, its gentle quest.

The rhythm flows, a steady stream,
Of hopes and fears, a waking dream,
An echo of the lives we've led,
The moments shared, the words unsaid.

So listen to the heart's own beat,
In its echo, love's rhythm meet,
A timeless dance, a boundless art,
The echoes of the beating heart.

Romantic Cadence

In twilight's glow, the night unfolds,
A cadence soft, in hues of gold,
Where whispers blend in lover's song,
And hearts in harmony belong.

The moonlight casts a silver sheen,
On moments still, and dreams unseen,
In every pulse, love's rhythm sways,
Through night and dawn, and endless days.

In shadows' dance, two souls entwine,
A timeless bond, both yours and mine,
With every beat, a promise true,
In romantic cadence, love renews.

Beneath the stars, the world is still,
Yet hearts within, their joy fulfill,
In every touch, a silent pledge,
In soft embrace, on love's fine edge.

So let us dance to time's sweet flow,
In rhythmic steps, where lovers go,
In endless night, our hearts align,
In romantic cadence, souls combine.

Silhouettes of the Soul

In twilight's hush, shadows dance on walls,
Where whispers linger, echoing through halls.
Silent dreams in silver streams, they stroll,
Revealing silhouettes of the soul.

Night unveils a canvas, dark and deep,
Secrets held in places shadows keep.
From light to dark, the ebb and flow,
Marking paths where thoughts may go.

Contours shift as moonlight gently falls,
Illuminating truths that darkness calls.
Within each shape a story scrolls,
In the silhouettes of the soul.

Ephemeral and fleeting, shades entwine,
Tracing borders, blurred by time.
In shadows, hidden truths console,
Speaking softly to the soul.

Against the sky, as stars ignite,
Silhouettes dance in the quiet night.
With every breath and silent knoll,
We glimpse the essence of the soul.

Pigments of Promise

In dawn's embrace, the colors rise,
A palette painted in the skies.
Soft hues of hope in golden streams,
Awaken dreams and cherished themes.

With every stroke, a future gleams,
In pigments pure, where vision teems.
Rainbows arch through clouds and blue,
A tapestry of dreams anew.

Fields ablaze in vibrant rows,
Promise blooms where the wild wind blows.
Each petal bright, a whisper deep,
Of secrets that the heart shall keep.

Beneath the azure, wishes fly,
On wings of light, they climb the sky.
In every shade, a tale unfurls,
Of vibrant hopes within our worlds.

Through storm and calm, the colors blend,
A spectrum wide, no start, no end.
In every hue, a promise flows,
Of tomorrows lit by the dawn's soft glow.

Seasons of Affection

Spring awakens hearts anew,
With blossoms sweet and morning dew.
In tender whispers, love takes root,
In every kiss, affection's fruit.

Summer's warmth envelops all,
In golden glow and evening's call.
Passions burn with fierce delight,
In lovers' arms throughout the night.

Autumn brings a gentle sigh,
Where leaves of gold and amber lie.
In cozy nights and fireside beams,
Affection deepens, softly gleams.

Winter's chill may touch the day,
But love, undaunted, finds its way.
In frosty air and silent snow,
Affection's warmth begins to grow.

Through every season, love endures,
A timeless bond, forever pure.
In cycles vast, love's essence stays,
Embraced in nature's tender ways.

Heartfelt Harmonies

In melodies that softly sing,
Heartfelt harmonies take wing.
With every note, a story told,
In tones that glitter, pure as gold.

Strings of love in gentle strums,
Echoes where affection hums.
Resonance in souls combined,
Within the chords, our hearts entwined.

Piano keys in tender dance,
Each press a moment to enhance.
With rhythm, cadence found in time,
Unveiling love in every chime.

A symphony of whispered vows,
In crescendos, love allows.
Fading echoes, soft and slow,
Revealing depths where feelings grow.

In every song, a heart laid bare,
Harmony in love's sweet care.
Unified in perfect blend,
A timeless tune that has no end.

Heart's Hues

Through valleys deep, where shadows play,
The heart speaks soft, in hues of gray,
Yet in the night, a light is spun,
A spectrum bright, 'til dawn is won.

Red of passion, fierce and true,
Blue of sorrow, there's the clue,
Green of growth, in every breath,
Yellow hope, outshining death.

Purple whispers, wise and old,
Pink of dreams, so soft and bold,
Orange warmth, when days are cold,
White for peace, a truth untold.

Each hue dances in the soul,
Many colors, yet one whole,
The heart, a canvas, paint it free,
With every shade of you and me.

From dawn til dusk, emotions blend,
A masterpiece around the bend,
Heart's hues, forever they will sing,
The beauty of this living thing.

Stenciled Sentiments

In the silence, words take flight,
Leaving stencils in the night,
Tracing dreams in wisps of air,
Etching visions, bold and rare.

Love in letters, carved so deep,
Promises that memories keep,
Hope in every line is cast,
Like a shadow from the past.

Ink of twilight, fills the mind,
Stories written, left behind,
Pages flutter, whisper low,
Tales that only hearts will know.

Sentiments in shadows graced,
Feelings held, yet not erased,
In the stencils, life revealed,
Secrets that remain concealed.

Drawn in silence, hearts align,
In the verses, we define,
Stenciled words, forever strong,
Echoes of our silent song.

Dappled Devotion

In a forest, calm and green,
Dappled light, a golden sheen,
Whispers sweet in every bough,
Nature's love, here and now.

Touched by sun and kissed by rain,
Devotion in the growing grain,
Leaves that flutter with the breeze,
Endless dance amid the trees.

Shadows play on fields of gold,
Stories of the earth retold,
In the roots and in the sky,
Devotion in each hue and sigh.

Streams that murmur soft and clear,
Songs of love for those who hear,
Hearts that echo nature's rhyme,
In devotion, lost in time.

Dappled light on life's great stage,
Seasons blend, page by page,
In our souls, a forest thrives,
With devotion, all survives.

Fragmented Feelings

Shattered whispers, soft and frail,
In the night, their echoes pale,
Scattered hopes across the sky,
Fragmented feelings can't deny.

Pieces lost in winds that turn,
Memories that silently yearn,
In each fragment, love remains,
Woven through life's tender pains.

Glimmers in the twilight's spread,
Dreams once held, now gently bled,
From the cracks, a light may beam,
Fragmented feelings still can dream.

In the broken, beauty hides,
Truth revealed in tear-filled tides,
Every piece a story tells,
Of love's fragmented, haunting spells.

Gathered shards, a heart remakes,
In the mending, darkness quakes,
From the fragments, strength is found,
Building life on sacred ground.

Ephemeral Emotions

In fleeting moments, hearts entwine,
A dance of whispers, pure, divine,
Ephemeral as morning dew,
Love's true essence, fresh and new.

A sigh, a touch, a fleeting glance,
Within these moments, souls enhance,
Ephemeral like clouds that drift,
From heart to heart, our spirits lift.

Through time's embrace, these feelings glide,
Ephemeral waves, an ocean wide,
In every heartbeat, stories told,
A love that's worth its weight in gold.

As stars align and shadows blend,
Ephemeral vows we do intend,
Each moment past, a cherished frame,
Though brief, they set our hearts aflame.

In fleeting kisses, love abides,
Ephemeral, where secrets hide,
Found in the spaces, light and dark,
The brief, the bright, our tender spark.

Love's Light Spectrum

A prism's light, a wondrous gleam,
Love shines in hues, a radiant dream,
From violet whispers, tender sighs,
To ruby passions in our eyes.

Emerald memories, laughter's glow,
In golden days, our hearts bestow,
Turquoise tides, where teardrops blend,
Love's spectrum means there's no end.

Saffron sunsets, warm embrace,
Each color holds a lover's grace,
In spectrum's dance, our spirits find,
A love evocative, yet kind.

Through sepia shades, though times may test,
Love's true hues shine their very best,
In hues of night and morning light,
Each color tells of our delight.

Cerulean skies, our hopes take flight,
Love's light spectrum, pure and bright,
In every shade, a story new,
Endless colors, endless truths.

Rhapsody of Roses

In gardens deep where roses bloom,
A rhapsody of sweet perfume,
Each petal sings a soft refrain,
Of tender love and gentle gain.

Crimson hues in morning's glow,
Love's passion in their bloom does show,
Roses dance in sunlight's kiss,
A symphony of purest bliss.

Through thorny paths, our hearts do strive,
In rhapsodies, our dreams arrive,
Each rose a note in love's grand song,
Together where we both belong.

Rosebuds promise, future bright,
In twilight's calm and silver light,
Rhapsodies of colors blend,
In roses, love does never end.

Petals falling, tender grace,
A sweet rhapsody to embrace,
In gardens where our spirits meet,
The rose's song, our hearts repeat.

Touch of Tenderness

With every touch, a gentle sway,
A love that finds its own sweet way,
Through tender moments softly shared,
Our hearts, in whispers, unprepared.

A brush of fingers, light and fine,
The world stands still, your hand in mine,
In tenderness, we carve our space,
A touch that time cannot erase.

Soft embraces, warm and kind,
A tenderness our souls define,
In every moment, pure delight,
A love that feels forever right.

Through silken threads, our stories spun,
In tenderness, we are as one,
No words, just echoes of our hearts,
In gentle touch, our love imparts.

With every kiss, our spirits rise,
In tender touch, we find the skies,
A whisper soft, a love so true,
In every touch, it's me and you.

Dreamscapes of Devotion

In realms where twilight dances, pure,
Soft whispers weave through night obscure,
With hearts aligned, in unity,
We tread the paths of serenity.

Stars imbue the canvas wide,
With dreams that shimmer, side by side,
In every breath, a sacred vow,
As time dissolves in here and now.

By moonlit lakes our souls converge,
In silent waves, emotions surge,
Through tender echoes, love's refrain,
We wander through devotion's gain.

Beneath the heavens' gentle gaze,
Our spirits bloom in endless praise,
In timeless fields of fervent dreams,
We float upon celestial streams.

Through stardust veils, we journey on,
With every dusk, another dawn,
In love's embrace, eternally,
We cherish dreamscapes' reverie.

Soulful Sceneries

In meadows kissed by morning's grace,
A soul finds solace, warm embrace,
With every hue, and fragrant breeze,
The heart's true essence, there it sees.

Beneath the ancient oak's wide arms,
A world unfolds with whispered charms,
In rustling leaves and gentle sighs,
The spirit soars where beauty lies.

Through fields of gold and skies of blue,
Each step reveals a vista new,
In tranquil lakes' reflective sheen,
The soul's own depth is softly seen.

Soft melodies of nature's choir,
Ignite within a fervent fire,
In every song, a story told,
In soulful sceneries, hearts unfold.

Where wildflowers paint the hill,
And rivers flow, serene and still,
In nature's art, a pure reprise,
Of dreams and hopes, and endless skies.

The Enchanted Palette

With brushes dipped in twilight's hue,
A masterpiece begins anew,
On canvas broad, the colors swirl,
And magic starts to gently twirl.

In strokes of green and shades of red,
A forest dream begins to spread,
Through dappled light and shadows deep,
An enchanted world we softly reap.

With every tint and every glow,
A myriad tales begin to flow,
From azure skies to golden sands,
Art breathes life with deft commands.

The hues of dusk, a symphony,
Of whispers told in mystery,
In painted wings, where hope takes flight,
An endless dance of dark and light.

Through artist's eye, the world transforms,
In all its hues, in all its forms,
On enchanted palette's vivid sheen,
Life blooms in colors yet unseen.

Delicate Dwelling

In chambers wrought with tender care,
A heart finds refuge, nestled there,
With every echo, soft and sweet,
A sanctum formed where souls may meet.

Through curtains light, the morning creeps,
In gentle whispers, daylight peeps,
With every beam, a promise cast,
To hold the present, not the past.

Beneath the eaves, in quiet grace,
A haven blooms, a sacred space,
Each corner whispers vows of peace,
In delicate dwelling, worries cease.

Within those walls, a garden grows,
Where love and laughter freely flows,
In petals soft and vines that climb,
Life's moments dance in rhythmic time.

In every room, a tale unfurls,
Of kindred souls and precious pearls,
In this abode, so pure, so true,
A delicate dwelling, built for two.

Flecks of Fondness

In twilight's gentle, glowing hue,
Flecks of fondness softly fall,
The memories that we once knew,
In whispers hear the night's sweet call.

Stars shall weave their silken tales,
Softly painting skies of old,
Where our laughter never pales,
In the warmth of love's strong hold.

Echoes of our secret dreams,
Dance within the evening air,
Love in corners softly gleams,
Found in moments pure and rare.

Hand in hand, we journey on,
Through the fields of yesteryear,
Drawn by love's eternal song,
No fear, no doubt, and no tear.

Tonight, beneath the starry shroud,
Hints of magic, time does wind,
In each fleck, a love avowed,
Fondness casts our hearts entwined.

Pen and Passion

Ink upon this parchment white,
Dreams and wishes, tales untold,
Passion spills in darkest night,
Words like embers, burning bold.

Stroke by stroke, the mind takes flight,
Crafting worlds from whispers low,
With each line, the heart ignites,
Passion's journey starts to grow.

Pens may falter, hands may tire,
Yet the spark remains alight,
Boundless realms and fierce desire,
Kindled in the hush of night.

Through each story, life anew,
Characters with hearts that gleam,
In the ink, a love so true,
Flowing like a fervent stream.

In this dance of pen and fire,
Dreams and passions intertwine,
As the writer's heart aspires,
Immortality in line.

The Color of Us

In hues of morning's golden kiss,
We paint the dawn with shades of hope,
Our lives, a canvas, endless bliss,
Blending colors, hearts elope.

Each stroke in love's embrace,
Crimson, blue, and tender green,
A masterpiece in sacred space,
A palette where our souls convene.

Under skies of twilight gray,
Our hues intensify and blend,
In the spectrum of our day,
Vivid tones until the end.

Through the streaks of rain and sun,
Every shade speaks truths and lies,
In each color, we are one,
Bound beneath the same vast skies.

From the dawn to setting sun,
Every hue reflects our trust,
In the tapestry we've spun,
Lives the color, the color of us.

Heartstrings in Shades

Notes that wander in the breeze,
Heartstrings plucked in soft accord,
Whispered dreams of melodies,
Each shade a love, a curtain floored.

Through the twilight's gentle veil,
Every strum reveals a story,
Shades of love, of joy, of frail,
Crafting moments transitory.

Strings of hope and tender grace,
Merge in rhythms pure and deep,
In each note, a warm embrace,
Lullabies that dare to weep.

Songs of mornings fresh and bright,
And of dusks that softly fade,
In this symphony of light,
All our shades, in love, parade.

Through the chords of joy and sorrow,
Heartstrings play their sweet charades,
Love endures, seeks no tomorrow,
In this dance of tender shades.

Pastel Passions

Gentle hues that softly blend,
In twilight's grasp, where dreams ascend.
Whispers of colors, pale and light,
A canvas kissed by the moon's soft might.

Blush of peach and lavender's sigh,
Soft as a lover's gentle lullaby.
Mint and sky in tranquil measure,
Crafting scenes of subtle pleasure.

Hands of dusk, sculpting grace,
In pastel shades, they find their place.
Delicate strokes, emotions weave,
In this realm, our hearts deceive.

A melody of pastel themes,
Woven deep in our quiet dreams.
Tender touches, crafted fine,
In pastel passions, love does shine.

Infused with Intimacy

Beneath the moon, our secrets share,
In quiet whispers, love laid bare.
A touch, a glance, so deeply felt,
In moments where our barriers melt.

Night's embrace, so warm and tender,
Where hearts in silence seek to render.
Stories told through fingertips,
In kisses soft as lovers' scripts.

Eyes that speak without a word,
In intimacy, truth is heard.
A bond that's forged in silent prayer,
In twilight's hush, our souls laid bare.

Grasping tightly, heart to heart,
Infused with intimacy, we start.
To weave our lives in tight embrace,
A tapestry of love and grace.

Charming Canvases

A stroke of blue, a hint of green,
In painted dreams, our souls convene.
Each brush's kiss, a tale unfolds,
Of stories rich and hues so bold.

Earthly tones and skies collide,
On charming canvases, we confide.
Each color speaks in silent chants,
In pigments' dance, our hearts enchant.

Brush and palette, born of dreams,
In every stroke, our essence gleams.
Through every hue, emotions flow,
In art's embrace, our spirits grow.

These charming canvases we fill,
With every fervent, fleeting thrill.
A spectrum wide of love and loss,
On each canvas, we emboss.

Brushstrokes of Emotion

In every stroke, a story lies,
Of hidden truths and heartfelt ties.
Colors blend where feelings meet,
In brushstrokes soft, and bittersweet.

Joy in yellow, sorrow in blue,
Each hue conveys a point of view.
Red for passion, green for hope,
Our hearts on canvas, learn to cope.

With every sweep, emotions sway,
In vibrant hues, we find our way.
From darkened nights to light's embrace,
With paint, we trace our heartfelt race.

A dance of colors intertwined,
In every stroke, our souls unwind.
Brushstrokes of emotion blend,
In art, our journeys find no end.

Rendered Sentiments

In shades of deep, emotions blend,
Across the canvas dreams extend.
Where whispers of the heart transcend,
A world of colors apprehend.

With every stroke, a feeling blooms,
In vibrant reds and silent plumes.
The soul expressed within the rooms,
And love's soft echoing perfumes.

The artist's hand, a gentle guide,
Through seas of blue and waves inside.
A journey where the thoughts reside,
In hues where truth and beauty bide.

Eyes that see beyond the frame,
In subtle tones, the light's acclaim.
Where every touch becomes a flame,
And memories invoke a name.

Rendered sentiment in silent hue,
A symphony of thoughts in view.
The paints and lines and space renew,
A dance of hearts in colors true.

Spectrum of Sensation

The dawning light, a spectrum bright,
Awakes the world in sheer delight.
With hues that blend and shades ignite,
A tapestry of pure insight.

In golden rays, sensations thrive,
Across the skies of morning drive.
Every touch and every strive,
In colors rich, emotions dive.

The purple dusk in velvet trim,
Where whispered dreams and hopes swim.
A canvas vast where stars bloom dim,
The night bestows in twilight hymn.

Every hue, a feeling's grace,
A touch, a glance within the space.
Where love's embrace in vivid trace,
Reflects the soul's expansive place.

Through light and dark, the senses range,
In every shade, the feelings change.
A spectrum vast, emotions strange,
In hues and tones, our lives arrange.

Heartfelt Fresco

Upon the wall, a tale unfolds,
In brush and stroke, a love untold.
Through swirling shades and colors bold,
A fresco blooms from ages old.

A heart depicted, tender, true,
In reds and golds, and deepest blue.
A dance of lines that softly cue,
The memories that time accrue.

Through shadows cast and lights that gleam,
A story woven, like a dream.
In every curve and every seam,
A whisper of a soft regime.

The fresco speaks in silence loud,
Of passions shared and hearts unbowed.
In every hue, the feelings crowd,
A tribute to the love avowed.

Heartfelt fresco, timeless art,
Of love that never will depart.
In painted dreams, the souls impart,
A masterpiece of the heart.

Introspective Portrait

The mirror holds a secret place,
Where inner worlds reveal their trace.
In quiet gaze, the thoughts embrace,
A portrait of the soul's own face.

With every line, the heart is drawn,
In shadows light and moments gone.
Reflections of the dawn at dawn,
Where hopes and fears together spawn.

Eyes that see beyond the veil,
In whispers soft, the truths unveil.
A silent journey to assail,
The inner storms and calm detail.

Through calm and chaos, all aligned,
The portrait forms within the mind.
A nexus where the self defined,
Emerges from the thoughts confined.

Introspective, deep and wide,
In painted strokes, the visions bide.
A portrait where the truths reside,
Of self within the time and tide.

Intangible Desires

In dreams of yesteryear, we sought
A realm where shadows softly danced.
Beyond the tangible, we fought,
To grasp what vanished at a glance.

Whispers echo in the night,
Secrets woven from the stars.
Yearning hearts take silent flight
To realms that shimmering hope unbars.

Through veils of mist, the path unseen,
We chase the phantoms of our fires.
The heart's deep longings crisply keen,
In chase of intangible desires.

With every breath, a farther reach,
Into the void, our spirits strive.
Beyond the known, where hearts beseech,
In dreams, we find we are alive.

Whispered winds that softly stir,
The world within, a mystic quest.
Through hazy mists, our visions blur,
Yet in that haze, we find our rest.

Passionate Palette

A canvas stretched, the colors bloom,
In hues that blaze with ardent song.
Passion's dance within the room,
A symphony where hearts belong.

Brushstrokes bold with fervent fire,
Each splash a tale of love's embrace.
From crimson's depth to gold's aspire,
The palette holds a timeless grace.

In twilight's shade, the pigments blend,
With purples deep and blues serene.
As fiery tones with shadows mend,
A masterpiece on life's wide screen.

With every stroke, a heartbeat's thrum,
The canvas breathes a living dream.
In passionate hues, creations hum,
As art and passion intertwine in gleam.

The palette of our souls displayed,
In colors bold and soft anew.
A testament of love portrayed,
In shades both fiery and true.

Throbbing Tapestry

Threads that weave an endless dance,
A tapestry of life unfurled.
Each heartbeat marks a brief romance,
In the fabric of the world.

Golden strands of sunlight weave,
Through silver shadows of the night.
A throb, a pulse, they interleave,
In patterns traced in flashing light.

Mystic threads of fate entwine,
With tapestries of joy and strife.
In every stitch, the stars align,
To tell the tale of mortal life.

With hands that guide the needle's flight,
We stitch our dreams in colors bold.
A throbbing dance of dark and light,
As mysteries and truths unfold.

In every weave, a story's spun,
Of love, of loss, of hope reborn.
A throbbing tapestry begun,
At dawn anew, til breath is worn.

Velvet Vulnerabilities

In shadows deep, where whispers creep,
A heart exposed, its guard undone.
Soft tears reveal, wounds concealed,
Beneath the moon, two souls as one.

Velvet nights, where secrets lie,
Glimmers faint, in silence high.
A fragile sway, in tender hold,
Stories old, and dreams untold.

Glimpse of truth, in a fleeting tear,
Eyes lament, what shadows cheer.
A dance of faith, in vulnerability,
Love's silent song, within reality.

Whispers brush against the veil,
Soothing tones that hearts impale.
In tender touch, a trust regains,
Soft caresses, mending chains.

At dawn's first light, the wounds will heal,
Binding trust in every seal.
In vulnerabilities, strength is found,
Love's soft murmur, echoes unbound.

Symphony of Shades

In twilight's grace, colors unfurl,
Notes of the night, in soft earl.
Dusk whispers tales of dark and bright,
A symphony of shades takes flight.

Echoes of stars in velvet skies,
Soft lullabies, where silence lies.
Moonlight weaves through shadows dense,
Harmony found in feeling immense.

Chords of dusk, in mellow tune,
Softly guiding the silver moon.
A canvas painted, night and dawn,
Pure symphony, love reborn.

Pale hues blend with starlit eyes,
Symphonic tones in night's disguise.
In every note, a secret sings,
Night's gentle pull, heartstrings it brings.

As morning calls with tender gaze,
Night's song departs in golden haze.
But in our hearts, the echoes stay,
Symphonic shades, forever play.

Canvas of Connection

Upon the canvas, strokes combine,
A dance of lines, so clear, divine.
Every hue a story starts,
Blending souls, with kindred hearts.

Colors merge, in passion's blend,
Each curve, a message, pathways send.
A touch of red, where hearts align,
Golden threads, softly entwine.

In quiet strokes, emotions speak,
Each shade, a tale, both strong and meek.
Connection deep, in every hue,
A silent bond, both old and new.

Brushes glide, with tender might,
Crafting love, from day to night.
Unspoken words, on canvas lie,
In art, our spirits unify.

Final stroke, a bond complete,
A masterpiece of hearts that meet.
In every line, connection's grace,
A timeless love, in painted space.

Heartbeats on Canvas

Hear the rhythm, soft and clear,
Brushes dance, a love revere.
Colors pulse with every beat,
Heartbeats on canvas, pure and sweet.

Soft strokes blend, in hues of red,
Every line a tale unsaid.
Whispers of the heart's true call,
In painted form, emotions scrawl.

Silent murmurs, through each shade,
Hidden dreams in colors laid.
Palette sings of love's embrace,
Heartbeats paint, with tender grace.

Every curve, a breath of life,
Art transcends both joy and strife.
In each blend, a pulse is felt,
Heartbeats weave, as colors melt.

As love's refrain on canvas stays,
Brushes hum in tranquil ways.
A painted symphony, hearts align,
In every beat, a love divine.

Reflections in Red

In the glow of twilight's thread,
Lies a world in hues of red.
Scarlet whispers soft and bright,
Paint the canvas of the night.

Amber skies begin to blend,
With crimson dreams that never end.
Roses bloom in fervent shade,
Dreams of passion softly laid.

In the flare of ruby's kiss,
Eclipsed moments bathe in bliss.
Hearts alight in fervid gleam,
Held within a scarlet dream.

Mirrored lakes of wine-hued sheen,
Reflect a world where love has been.
Crimson waves and crimson wind,
Echo where the heart begins.

Endless realms where reds resound,
In reflections love is found.
Scarlet sighs and ruby sparks,
Kindle flames in shadowed dark.

Cerulean Affections

Azure skies with endless waves,
Whisper soft in ocean's caves.
Hearts as blue as morning's hue,
In the softness find what's true.

Tides of blue in silent roll,
Touch the very depths of soul.
Lap against the shores of night,
Cerulean affections light.

Whispers carried on the breeze,
Calm the restless, lift with ease.
In the expanse of the blue,
Love is found so strong, so true.

Waves of sapphire years unfold,
Tales of love so deeply told.
In the depths where dreams reside,
Cerulean hearts confide.

Skies that meld with ocean's crest,
Sing of love that finds its rest.
In the arms of blue's embrace,
Heart and soul in quiet grace.

Amber Embers

Golden sun in twilight's hold,
Spills its treasures, bright and bold.
In the hue of amber light,
Embers glow throughout the night.

Stars ignite in amber's gaze,
Casting warmth through evening's haze.
Flames that dance in mellow gold,
Ancient tales of love retold.

In the flicker, shadows play,
Beneath the amber's gentle sway.
Softly weaving dreams anew,
In the light of amber's view.

Autumn leaves in amber hue,
Whisper secrets, old and true.
Timeless love in fires kindled,
Hearts with amber softly mingled.

Golden moments, warmth and peace,
In the night, the worries cease.
In the glow of amber's gleam,
Love is found in softest dream.

Cobalt Confessions

Midnight skies of deepest blue,
Hold the secrets, old and new.
In the cobalt, whispers hide,
Confessions made in quiet tide.

Waves that match the darkened sky,
Surge with truths we can't deny.
In the depths of cobalt's hold,
Heartfelt stories gently told.

Azure dreams in twilight's fall,
Hear the cobalt's silent call.
Promises in shadows cast,
Linger in the moments past.

In the night where blue prevails,
Cobalt winds tell tender tales.
Starlit skies with silent glow,
Hold the love we seldom show.

Endless tides of deepened hue,
Wash upon the shores of blue.
In the cobalt's gentle grace,
Hold confessions we embrace.

Textures of Tenderness

Soft whispers brushed in twilight's hush,
A feathered touch, a gentle push,
Embracing warmth in night's contour,
Love's textures lay, serene and pure.

Hands like silk, tracing dreams,
In tender loops, the starlight beams,
Hearts entwined like morning dew,
In tender textures, love renews.

Velvet words on lips of grace,
Each syllable, a soft embrace,
In the quietude, we find our song,
Textures of tenderness, where we belong.

Caresses light as butterfly wings,
In this dance, the heart softly sings,
A tapestry of moments shared,
In tender textures, none compared.

Through whispered winds and shadows slight,
We weave our love in tender light,
In every touch, a story spun,
Textures of tenderness, forever as one.

Soul's Portrait

Painted skies with hues so grand,
Silent strokes by life's fair hand,
In every shade, the soul's intent,
A portrait of the heart's lament.

Through colors bright and shadows deep,
Emotions raw, no secrets keep,
Each brush's kiss on canvas pure,
Reveals a soul both strong and sure.

The crimson of the heart's desire,
Set ablaze by passion's fire,
Gentle blues of tranquil times,
Form the soul's poetic rhymes.

Golden streaks of fleeting joy,
Moments cherished, never coy,
In each corner, stories hide,
In the soul's portrait, far and wide.

In every stroke, a life unfolds,
A tale of love, and dreams untold,
A masterpiece, both bold and frail,
Soul's portrait, its own grand tale.

Impressions of Intimacy

Glimpses caught in time's embrace,
An intimate world of tender grace,
Moments brushed with love's sweet hue,
Impressions of intimacy, ever true.

Soft sighs in whispered night,
Hearts entwined in love's soft light,
In the space where shadows play,
Intimacy deepens, come what may.

Gentle moments, fleeting, rare,
A touch, a glance, love laid bare,
In the quietude of a shared space,
Intimacy's impressions leave their trace.

Eyes that speak what words can't tell,
In their depths, emotions swell,
A silent dance of souls entwined,
Impressions of intimacy, undefined.

In every look, a promise kept,
In every touch, a vow we've wept,
Intimacy's impressions, pure and free,
Are the heart's deepest tapestry.

Charcoal Confessions

On parchment pale, the charcoal sighs,
Sketches born where truth lies,
In shadows dark and lines so bold,
Charcoal confessions quietly told.

Every stroke, a whispered secret,
In each curve, our souls beget,
Truths entwined in ebony's flow,
Confessions in a subtle glow.

Textures rough, yet stories smooth,
In charcoal's grace, our hearts groove,
Darkened dreams and whispered fears,
Confessions drawn through time's tears.

Each line etched with hope's refrain,
In charcoal's embrace, we meet again,
Through the dark, a light unveiled,
Confessions of a heart unscaled.

Ephemeral, yet forever marked,
Charcoal confessions, love's stark art,
In the blackness, the soul reveals,
Truths and dreams that charcoal seals.

Resonant Brushstrokes

In whispers of hues, a story is spun,
Canvas awash in twilight's soft glow.
Each stroke a sigh, each hue a sonnet,
Heartbeats echo where pigments flow.

Soft blues meld with passionate reds,
Creating a symphony on linen spread.
Mysteries whispered by the artist's hand,
Dreamscapes born where colours blend.

Veins of gold trace evening skies,
Twilight's breath, a tender brush.
In silent dance, the hues confide,
A painter's love, in every touch.

Emerald meadows and sapphire streams,
Captured within an artist's dreams.
Resonating beauty, life unfolds,
In every drop, a tale retold.

Endless muse in every glance,
Creation bound in painter's trance.
Their heart reflects in vibrant waves,
Resonant strokes, eternal staves.

Melody of Memories

Soft echoes of a distant song,
Remind us where we once belonged.
Melodies weave through time's embrace,
Carving paths in memory's space.

Notes cascade like autumn leaves,
Whispers of love that never leaves.
Harmony of laughter, chords of tears,
Music spun from fleeting years.

Verse by verse, a past unfurled,
In gentle rhythms, dawns a world.
Voices linger in twilight's air,
Carrying tales beyond compare.

Strings of moments finely plucked,
In heart's chest, serenades tucked.
A requiem of days gone by,
Soft refrains beneath the sky.

The melody fades but never dies,
Echoing through life's evening skies.
A symphony of what was dear,
In every note, our yesteryear.

Celestial Sculptures

In night's embrace, the stars align,
Crafting tales in silver shine.
Each constellation whispers low,
Chiseling stories in cosmic glow.

Galaxies as marble skies,
Twinkling carvings before our eyes.
Celestial hands mold light and shade,
Eternal art in heavens laid.

Planets drift in an astral dance,
Spiraled forms in vast expanse.
Orbits carved by cosmic blades,
Luminous paths that time pervades.

Nebulae as sculptor's clay,
Ethereal forms in night display.
In swirling hues, life's breath concealed,
Starry sculptures thus revealed.

Beyond the reach of mortal hands,
Creation rests in distant strands.
Celestial legacies etched in light,
In heaven's gallery, pure and bright.

Intimate Symphony

In twilight hush, a whisper starts,
Melodies played by tender hearts.
Soft symphony of love's own weave,
Two souls in harmony, interleave.

Notes entwined in lovers' grace,
A duet in a sacred space.
Breathes and sighs where music lives,
A song that only true love gives.

Fingers trace the silent keys,
Crafting tunes in gentle breeze.
Heartstrings strummed in time's embrace,
A timeless waltz, a cherished place.

Eyes that sing in silent prose,
Lyrics felt where feeling grows.
Symphony intimate, pure and rare,
Love composed in whispered air.

Forever echoes in lovers' ears,
A tune that conquers fleeting years.
Intimate symphony, deeply sown,
Where hearts unite and love is known.

Canvas of My Soul

In the silence of night's embrace,
Brushstrokes whisper in gentle grace.
Stars paint dreams across the sky,
As shadows dance and spirits sigh.

Colors bleed from heart to hand,
Crafting worlds at love's command.
Each hue a tale, each stroke a song,
On this canvas, I belong.

Light and dark in swift ballet,
Mingle in the dawn's early gray.
In every line, a story told,
On the canvas of my soul.

Textures weave, emotions blend,
Echoing whispers that never end.
Truth and dreams in vibrant gleam,
This, my eternal dream.

With every touch, with every hue,
I share my heart, my essence, true.
The canvas holds what words can't paint,
A love unending, free from taint.

Symphony of Feelings

Notes drift softly on the breeze,
Whispers of the heart with ease.
Melodies tender, harmonies sweet,
In this symphony, our souls meet.

Strings of passion, winds of grace,
A dance of love through time and space.
Chords of longing, beats of joy,
A symphony time can't destroy.

In every measure, in every rhyme,
Echoes of a love, sublime.
Tunes that linger, songs that stay,
Guiding us through night and day.

Emotion's cadence, rhythm's flight,
A symphony born in love's light.
Voices blend in perfect tune,
Underneath a silver moon.

Through crescendos, through the calm,
We find shelter in this balm.
A symphony of feelings true,
A serenade of me and you.

Lyrical Pulses

Rhythms of the heart beat strong,
In every pulse, a whispered song.
Echoes of a love refined,
In harmony, our souls aligned.

Verses form in tender grace,
In each line, I see your face.
Lyrical pulses, heartbeats blend,
In this poem, we transcend.

Words that dance on lips of light,
Kissing shadows of the night.
In their cadence, truths are spun,
Binding two hearts into one.

With every heartbeat, verses flow,
In them, all our secrets show.
Lyrical pulses, love's refrain,
A song of joy amidst the rain.

In the meter, hope and fear,
In each stanza, you're always near.
A sonnet of us, tender seals,
In lyrical pulses, our love reveals.

Chromatic Love

In a palette rich with hues,
Love's true colors find their muse.
Violet dreams and sapphire skies,
In your eyes, my heart lies.

Crimson passion, emerald grace,
In each touch, a warm embrace.
Shades of love in endless blend,
Chromatic promises transcend.

Golden sunrises, twilight's blush,
In their glow, my heart does rush.
Colors weaving, threads entwined,
In this art, true love defined.

Each pigment tells a story bright,
Of days in love and stars at night.
Tones that whisper sweet and bold,
In chromatic arms, we hold.

From dawn to dusk, a spectrum wide,
In every shade, you're by my side.
Chromatic love, ever true,
In every color, I see you.

Sublime Strokes of Love

In the twilight's gentle embrace,
Two hearts beat in perfect grace.
Whispers soft as nightfall's dove,
Paint the strokes of boundless love.

Eclipsed by moon's tender glow,
Affection's stream begins to flow.
Canvas kissed by stars above,
Sublime strokes define our love.

Harmony in hues so bright,
Love's tune echoes in the night.
Colors blend in warm caress,
Forming shades of tenderness.

Brush upon the heartstrings played,
Memories in tones displayed.
Bound by fate, this art shall move,
Each stroke tells our tale of love.

In this gallery of dreams,
Light and love in endless streams.
Masterpiece we rise above,
Framed within our painted love.

Inkblots of Emotion

Drops of ink on paper wide,
Feelings flow we cannot hide.
Blots and splotches tell a tale,
Of emotions that prevail.

From the nib our sorrow slips,
Joyful cries at fingertips.
Ebon tears and laughter bright,
Spread like wings into the night.

Pages filled with love's refrain,
Echoes of inevitable pain.
Ink reveals what words conceal,
Depths of what we truly feel.

Each blot whispers silent screams,
Joy and heartache in our dreams.
Illustrations in the fray,
Ink reveals our night and day.

Emotion's ink on parchment stayed,
Ever in our hearts portrayed.
Artful blots, a tale in motion,
Life inscribed in raw emotion.

Brushes of the Soul

With gentle strokes and gentle sighs,
Soul paints pictures in the skies.
Every line and every shade,
Fragments of a life portrayed.

Brush in hand and heart alight,
Colors dance, a pure delight.
Memory and dreams unroll,
Through the brushes of the soul.

Painters of the inner mind,
Seeking beauty undefined.
Captured moments softly stole,
In the brushes of the soul.

Past and future gently blend,
Scenes of love they ever send.
Whispers through our lives extol,
In the brushes of the soul.

Each artwork a tale discerned,
From the lessons we have learned.
Canvas speaks what words control,
Life revealed by soul's great scroll.

Milton Keynes UK
Ingram Content Group UK Ltd.
UKHW020703090824
446663UK00012B/278

9 789916 863015